LIFE IN THE PAST

Victorian Schools

Mandy Ross

Raintree

www.raintreepublishers.co.uk
Visit our website to find out
more information about
Raintree books.

To order:
☎ Phone 0845 6044371
🖷 Fax +44 (0) 1865 312263
🖳 Email myorders@raintreepublishers.co.uk

Customers from outside the UK please telephone +44 1865 312262

Editorial: Lucy Thunder and Helen Cannons
Design: Steve Mead
Picture research: Rebecca Sodergren and
Liz Savery
Printed and bound in China by South China
Printing Company

ISBN 978 1 406 25187 6 (paperback)
15 14 13 12
10 9 8 7 6 5 4 3 2

**British Library Cataloguing in Publication
Data**
Ross, Mandy
Victorian schools. – (Life in the past)

A full catalogue record for this book is
available from the British Library.

Acknowledgements
We would like to thank the following for
permission to reproduce photographs: The Art
Archive/The Bodleian Library, Oxford p20;
The Art Archive, Musee d'Orsay, Paris/Dagli
Orti p9; Bridgeman Art Library/Christopher
Wood Gallery, London p12; Corbis p4;
Corbis/Edifice/Philippa Lewis p28; Corbis/
Hulton-Deutsch Collection p15; Corbis/Peter
Yates p7; Fine Art Photographic Library pp14,
21; Hulton Archive pp5, 6, 16, 24; Mary
Evans Picture Library pp8, 10, 19, 22, 23, 25,
27; Ragged School p29; Topham Picturepoint
pp11, 13, 17, 18; Victorian Library Images
p26.

Cover photograph of girls reading in school
in 1900 reproduced with permission of Billie
Love Historical Collection.

We would like to thank Jane Shuter for her
invaluable help in the preparation of this book.

Every effort has been made to contact
copyright holders of material reproduced in
this book. Any omissions will be rectified in
subsequent printings if notice is given to the
publishers.

Contents

Words written in bold, **like this**, are explained in the Glossary.

Who were the Victorians?

Queen Victoria **reigned** in Britain from 1837 to 1901. People who lived at this time are called Victorians. Some Victorians were very rich and others were very poor indeed.

This Victorian newspaper picture shows Queen Victoria visiting a girls' school.

Queen Victoria

Victorian life was very different from today. Many of our everyday things were not yet **invented** at the start of Victoria's reign. There were no cars, telephones or computers.

▼ This photograph from 1896 shows a horse-drawn bus and a motor bus in a busy London street.

motor bus

Schools then and now

At the beginning of Victoria's **reign**, many children got little or no schooling – especially the poor. By the end of Victoria's reign, children had to go to school until they were twelve.

Victorian schools were much stricter than today. Children had to sit in rows.

▲ Modern children in a science lesson.

School is much more fun today than it was in Victorian times. Now, children are free to explore and learn for themselves. What do you like doing best at school?

Little ladies

Most girls from rich families did
not go to school. They were taught
at home by a **governess** or **tutor**.
Sometimes their younger brothers
shared their lessons.

▼ This governess is reading to her pupils.

ink well

◀ This famous painting by Pierre-Auguste Renoir was painted in 1892. It shows two girls at the piano.

Many families thought that girls only needed a very basic education. They were mainly taught things they would need to attract a husband, such as singing, drawing and needlework.

Toughen them up!

Boys from rich families were sent away to **boarding school** from around the age of seven. Their lives were harsh and uncomfortable at school, to toughen them up.

▼ Boys in their shared bedroom, called a dormitory, at boarding school.

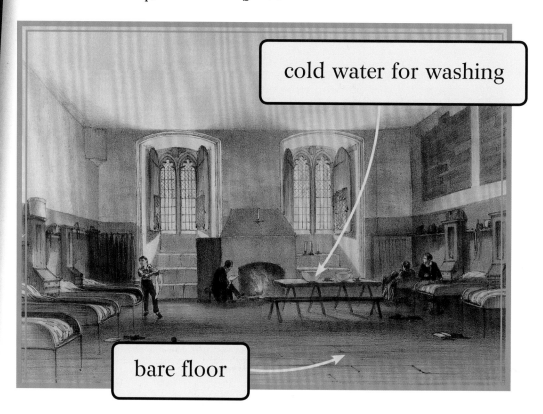

cold water for washing

bare floor

Many **middle-class** families sent their sons to local **grammar schools**. Boys were expected to work hard, be clean and neat, and to obey their teacher.

▼ No matter how boring the lesson, these boys had to pay attention or they would be punished.

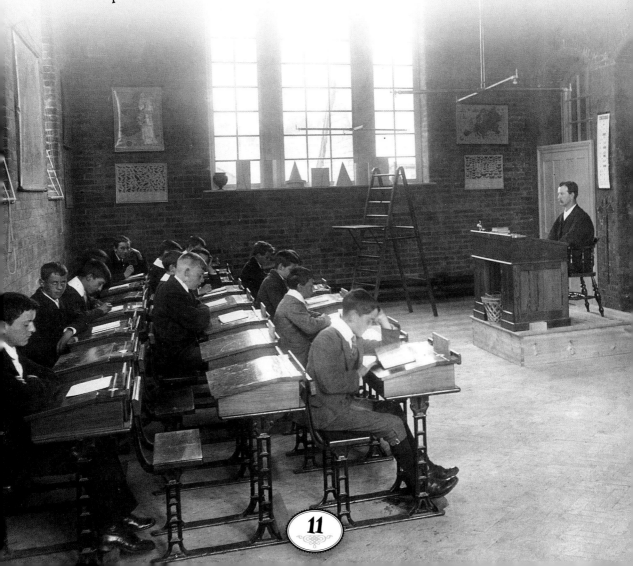

A little learning

Many families could not afford high **fees** charged by schools. From the 1830s, churches and **charities** set up schools with lower fees. Children learnt religion and the 'three Rs' – reading, writing and arithmetic (maths).

This woman is teaching children in her home. This might be all the schooling children would get.

Many poor families could not afford to send their children to school at all. They needed children to work from an early age, to bring money into the home.

Sunday school, ragged schools

Children who worked every day except Sunday could go to Sunday school at church. There they could learn as they read from the Bible.

▲ This painting, from 1874, shows a minister teaching at a Sunday school.

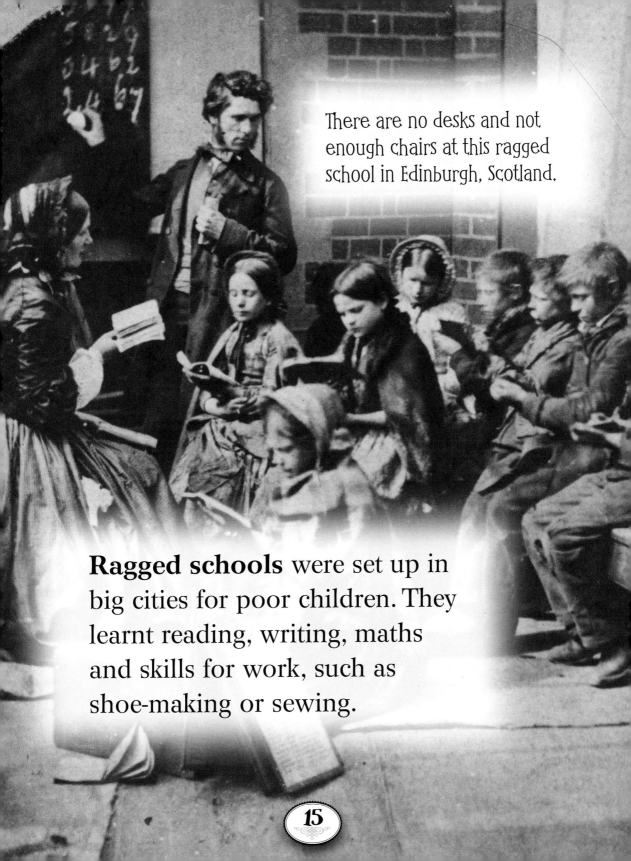

There are no desks and not enough chairs at this ragged school in Edinburgh, Scotland.

Ragged schools were set up in big cities for poor children. They learnt reading, writing, maths and skills for work, such as shoe-making or sewing.

School for all

In 1870, the government made new **laws** saying that all children from the age of five to ten could go to school. Many schools were built. Some had huge classes – with about 200 pupils.

▼ Older children called monitors are helping the teacher with this large class.

teacher

monitor

A new law in 1880 said all children had to go to school. Basic schooling became free for everyone in 1891. Children were then taught the 'three Rs', history, geography and a little science, too.

► After 1880, children who did not want to go to school were made to go.

In the classroom

Victorian teachers were very strict. Children had to behave well all the time. The teachers worked hard to teach such big classes.

▼ A boys' class photograph. The writing on the blackboard says, 'Do right and fear not'.

▶ This boy is standing on a stool and wearing a **dunce's hat** as a punishment.

There were harsh punishments for children who did not obey their teacher. Sometimes they were beaten for being naughty. Many children were afraid at school.

Learning lessons

What might you find in a Victorian classroom? Some objects might be familiar today, such as a chalkboard, map or globe. There were no calculators or computers, though.

This page from a Victorian picture book shows objects from the schoolroom.

Victorian children wrote by scratching on a slate. The **slate** could be wiped clean to use again. Mostly children learnt lessons by heart, or copied from the blackboard.

Here are some sayings which Victorian children might have copied:

'A fool and his money are soon parted.'

'Waste not, want not.'

Running around

Like other lessons, sport or PE was strict. Children stood in long lines in the playground to do exercises, called drill, together.

▼ These Victorian boys are doing exercises in a foggy school playground.

Victorian schools did not have playtime, like schools today. Children played together before and after school. There were no adults in charge, so bigger children often bullied smaller ones.

Learning for life

Once they were past the age of ten, the lives of rich and poor children became even more different. Children from richer families might go to **grammar schools**. A lucky few might go on to university.

▼ This school photograph from 1880 shows grammar school boys wearing medals for being good.

Poorer children learnt skills for work and life, such as woodwork or **laundry**. This was to help them to earn their living.

washing board

flat iron

laundry tubs

These girls are learning how to iron collars and cuffs in London.

Adults at school

Many adults who had not learnt much at school wanted to educate themselves. New, free public libraries were opened so that people could borrow books to read.

▲ The Victorian library in the town of Cheltenham is still in use today.

Trades unions, libraries and other organizations put on evening classes for adults. Many men and women learnt new skills and got better jobs.

slate

chalkboard

teacher

▲ A free evening class for working men in Louth, Lincolnshire.

Let's find out!

Many Victorian school buildings are still in use today. Can you find out when your school was built? Which schools in your area were built in Victorian times?

▲ Modern children playing outside their small Victorian school building.

▲ These school children are visiting the
Ragged School Museum in London to find
out what a ragged school was like.

You can find out more about Victorian
schools at your local library or museum.
Ask for information about Victorian
buildings to visit in your area.

Timeline

1833   Government starts school **inspections**

1837   Victoria is crowned Queen of Great Britain

1842   New **laws** stop children under ten from working underground in mines. Government starts to train pupils who want to be teachers while they are still at school.

1851   The Great Exhibition is held at the Crystal Palace, London

1854   British troops fight in the Crimean War against Russia

1861   Prince Albert, Victoria's husband, dies

1870   Government passes a law saying there should be enough schools for all children from the ages of five to ten to go to school. Government builds schools and employs teachers for the first time.

1880   All children between the age of five and ten have to go to school

1891   Free schooling provided for all children

1899   All children have to go to school until they are twelve years old

1901   Queen Victoria dies

Glossary

boarding school school which pupils live in during the week or the term

charities organizations that help and raise money for those in need

dunce's hat cone-shaped hat worn as a punishment for not doing well in lessons

fee payment charged

governess woman employed to teach and look after children in their own home

grammar school school which charges fees and pupils have to pass an exam to enter

inspection to take a close look at something

invent to make something a new way, or to find a new way of doing something

laundry washing clothes, bedding and other things

law rule made by parliament that everyone must obey

middle-class people who earn enough money to live comfortably, for instance doctors

ragged school Victorian school for poor children

reign to be the king or queen of a country, or the period a king or queen spends on the throne

slate flat piece of stone, used for writing on

trades union organization set up by workers to improve their pay, safety and rights at work

tutor person employed to teach children in their own home

Find out more

Books

A Victorian Childhood: At School, Ruth Thomson (Franklin Watts, 2007)

Be a History Detective: Victorian School, Susie Brooks (Wayland, 2009)

Starting History: The Victorians, Sally Hewitt (Franklin Watts, 2006)

Places and websites to visit

www.nationaltrust.org.uk
The National Trust has information about historic buildings to visit in your area.

www.vam.ac.uk/moc
You can learn more about Victorian childhood at the Museum of Childhood in London.

Index